T0128308

FIFTY-TWO WEEKS TO GROW

MEDITATE, COLOR, AND MEMORIZE
SCRIPTURE EACH WEEK OF THE YEAR

Illustrated by

ERIN SPARACINO

Copyright © 2020 Erin Sparacino.

All rights reserved. No part of this book may be used or reproduced by any means, graphic, electronic, or mechanical, including photocopying, recording, taping or by any information storage retrieval system without the written permission of the author except in the case of brief quotations embodied in critical articles and reviews.

This book is a work of non-fiction. Unless otherwise noted, the author and the publisher make no explicit guarantees as to the accuracy of the information contained in this book and in some cases, names of people and places have been altered to protect their privacy.

WestBow Press books may be ordered through booksellers or by contacting:

WestBow Press
A Division of Thomas Nelson & Zondervan
1663 Liberty Drive
Bloomington, IN 47403
www.westbowpress.com
844-714-3454

Because of the dynamic nature of the Internet, any web addresses or links contained in this book may have changed since publication and may no longer be valid. The views expressed in this work are solely those of the author and do not necessarily reflect the views of the publisher, and the publisher hereby disclaims any responsibility for them.

Scripture taken from the New King James Version®. Copyright © 1982 by Thomas Nelson. Used by permission. All rights reserved.

ISBN: 978-1-6642-0658-8 (sc)
ISBN: 978-1-6642-0659-5 (e)

Library of Congress Control Number: 2020918594

Print information available on the last page.

WestBow Press rev. date: 10/29/2020

"Thanks be to God for His indescribable gift!" 2 Corinthians 9:15

www.thisisyourbible.com
www.biblebasedbeliefs.com

Do you struggle to commit to heart God's word? This coloring book is a creative, family-friendly way to encourage the young and young at heart to enjoy and memorize Bible verses.

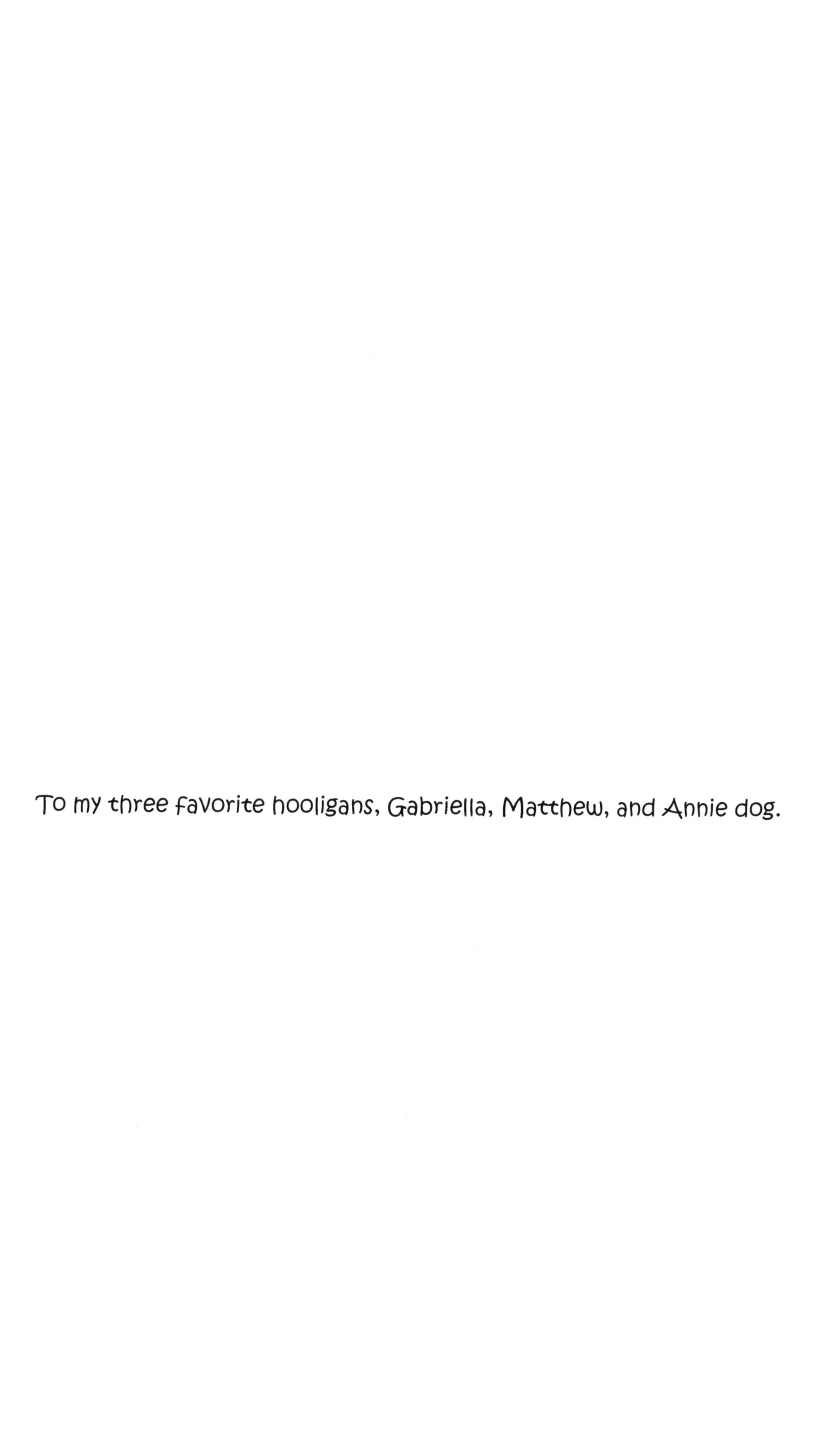

To my three favorite hooligans, Gabriella, Matthew, and Annie dog.

"For the earth will be filled with the knowledge of the glory of the LORD, as the waters cover the sea."

—Habakkuk 2:14

"Every good gift and every perfect gift is from above, and comes down from the Father of lights, with whom there is no variation or shadow of turning."

—James 1:17

"I will both lie down in peace and sleep; for You alone, O LORD, make me dwell in safety."

—Psalm 4:8

"Now abide faith, hope, love, these three; but the greatest of these is love."

—1 Corinthians 13:13

"Trust in the LORD with all your heart, and lean not on your own understanding. In all your ways acknowledge Him and He shall direct your paths."

—Proverbs 3:5-6

"Therefore, do not be anxious about tomorrow, for tomorrow will worry about its own things. Sufficient for the day is its own trouble."

—Matthew 6:34

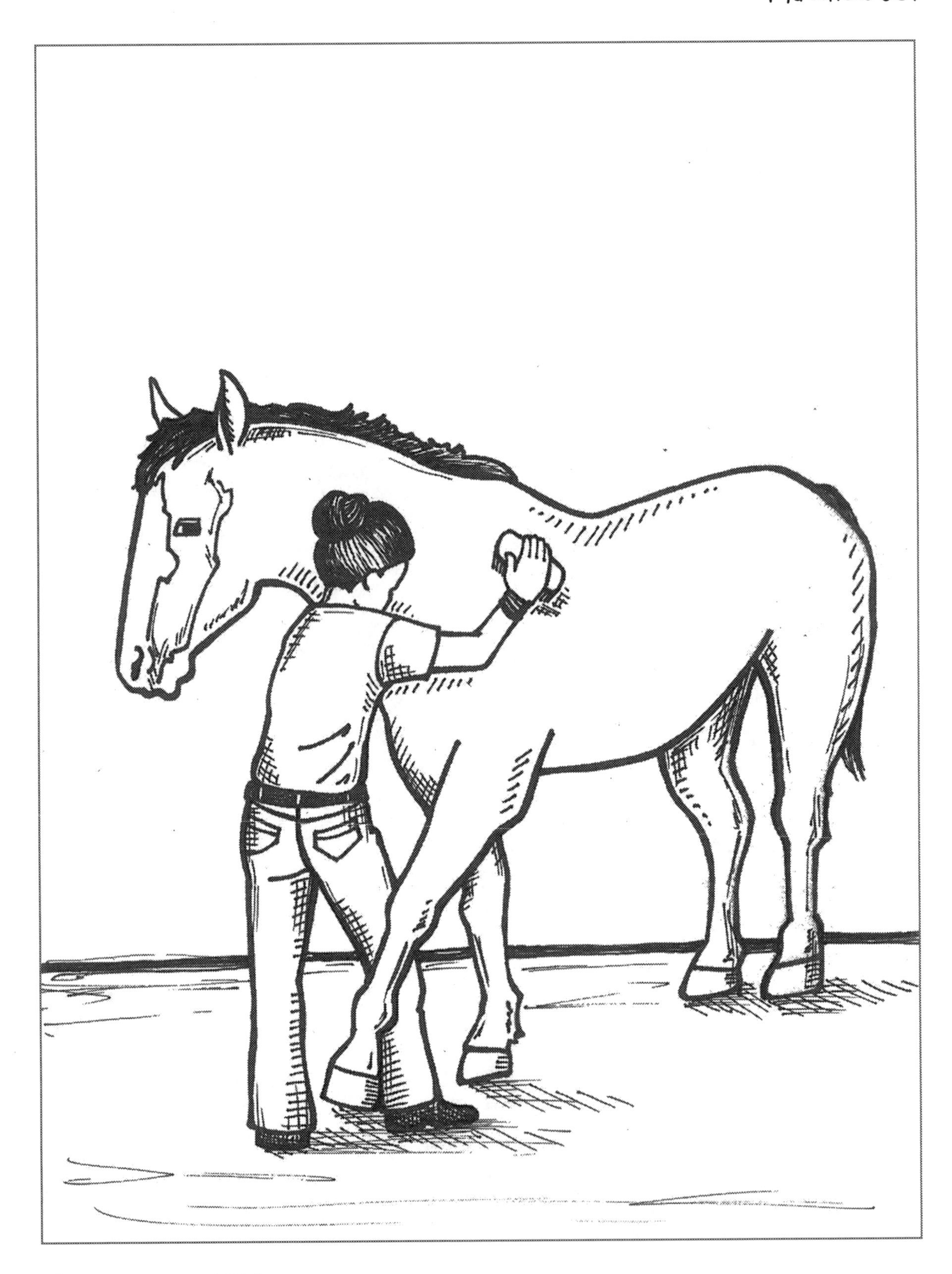

"All scripture is given by inspiration of God, and is profitable for doctrine, for reproof, for correction, for instruction in righteousness, that the man of God may be complete, equipped for every good work." —2 Timothy 3:16-17

"Be anxious for nothing, but in everything by prayer and supplication, with thanksgiving, let your requests be made known to God; and the peace of God, which surpasses all understanding will guard your hearts and minds through Christ Jesus."

—Philippians 4:6-7

"This is the day the LORD has made; We will rejoice and be glad in it."

—Psalm 118:24

"For where your treasure is, there your heart will also be."

—Matthew 6:21

"For You formed my inward parts; You covered me in my mother's womb. I will praise You, for I am fearfully and wonderfully made. Marvelous are Your works; and that my soul knows very well."

—Psalm 139:13-14

“But the fruit of the Spirit is love, joy, peace, long-suffering, kindness, goodness, faithfulness, gentleness, self-control.”

—Galatians 5:22-23

"For I know the thoughts that I think towards you, says the LORD, thoughts of peace and not of evil, to give you a future and a hope."

—Jeremiah 29:11

"For with God nothing will be impossible!"

—Luke 1:37

"But Jesus said, "Let the little children come to Me, and do not forbid them; for of such is the kingdom of heaven."

—Matthew 19:14

"A new commandment I give to you, that you love one another; as I have loved you, that you also love one another. By this all will know that you are My disciples, if you have love for one another."

—John 13:34-35

"But everyone shall sit under his vine and under his fig tree, and no one shall make them afraid, for the mouth of the LORD of hosts has spoken."

—Micah 4:4

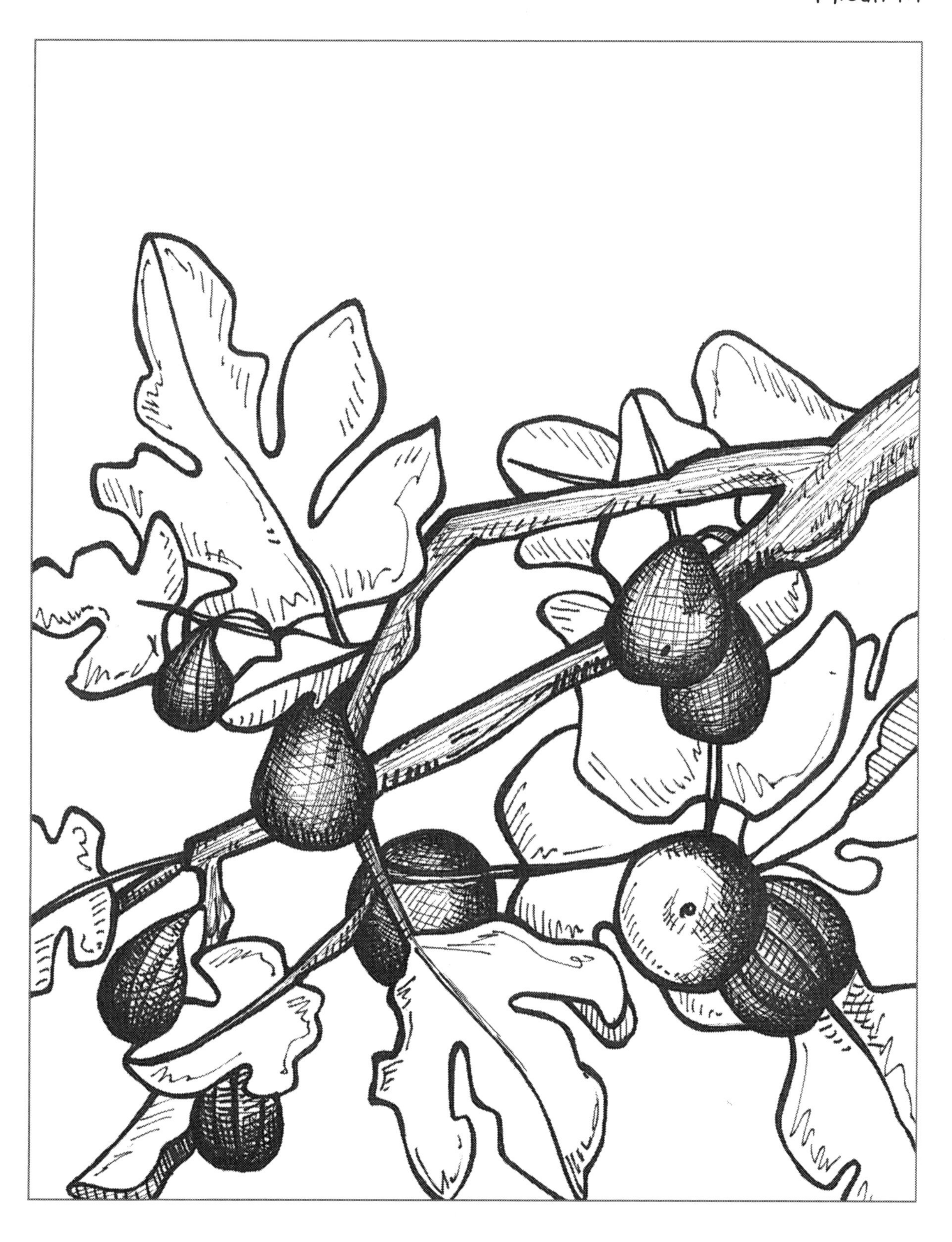

“He has shown you, O man, what is good; and what does the LORD require of you, but to do justly, to love mercy, and to walk humbly with your God?”

—Micah 6:8

"Children obey your parents in the LORD, for this is right. "Honor your father and mother," which is the first commandment with promise: that it may be well with you and you may live long on the earth."

—Ephesians 6:1-2

"The LORD is my light and my salvation, whom shall I fear? The LORD is the strength of my life, of whom shall I be afraid?"

—Psalm 27:1

"Have I not commanded you? Be strong and of good courage; do not be afraid, nor be dismayed, for the LORD your God is with you wherever you go."

—Joshua 1:9

"Create in me a clean heart, O God, and renew a steadfast spirit within me."

—Psalm 51:10

"I can do all things through Christ who strengthens me."

—Philippians 4:13

"You will keep him in perfect peace, whose mind is stayed on You, because he trusts in You."

—Isaiah 26:3

"He has made everything beautiful in its time ..."

—Ecclesiastes 3:11

"To everything there is a season, a time for every purpose under heaven."
—Ecclesiastes 3:1

"These things I have spoken to you, that in Me you may have peace. In the world you will have tribulation; but be of good cheer, I have overcome the world."

—John 16:33

"Blessed are those who do His commandments, that they may have the right to the tree of life and may enter through the gates into the city."

—Revelation 22:14

"Now faith is the substance of things hope for, the evidence of things not seen."

—Hebrews 11:1

"Two are better than one, because they have a good reward for their labor."

—Ecclesiastes 4:9

"Let nothing be done through selfish ambition or conceit, but in lowliness of mind let each esteem others better than himself."

—Philippians 2:3

"For I, the LORD your God, will hold your right hand, saying to you, 'Fear not, I will help you.'

—Isaiah 41:13

"...But as for me and my house, we will serve the LORD."

—Joshua 24:15

"...let every man be swift to hear, slow to speak, slow to wrath; for the wrath of man does not produce the righteousness of God."

—James 1:19-20

"Before I formed you in the womb, I knew you; before you were born, I sanctified you ..."

—Jeremiah 1:5

"But those who wait on the LORD will renew their strength; they shall mount up with wings like eagles; they shall run and not be weary; they shall walk and not faint."

—Isaiah 40:31

"Blessed is the man who endures temptation; for when he has been approved, he will receive the crown of life which the Lord has promised to those who love Him."

—James 1:12

"And we know that all things work together for good to those who love God, to those who are called according to His purpose."

—Romans 8:28

"Train up a child in the way he should go, and when he is old he will not depart from it."

—Proverbs 22:6

"...Hosanna to the Son of David! Blessed is He who comes in the name of the LORD! Hosanna in the highest!"

—Matthew 21:9

"When you lie down, you will not be afraid; yes, you will lie down and your sleep will be sweet."

—Proverbs 3:24

"Love … bears all things, believes all things, hopes all things, endures all things. Love never fails."

—1 Corinthians 13:7-8

"Let each of you look out not only for his own interests, but also for the interests of others."

—Philippians 2:4

"Hope deferred makes the heart sick, but when the desire comes, it is a tree of life."

—Proverbs 13:12

"The heavens declare the glory of God; and the firmament shows His handiwork."
—Psalm 19:1

"Wait on the LORD; be of good courage, and He shall strengthen your heart. Wait, I say, on the LORD!" —Psalm 27:14

"How sweet are your words to my taste, sweeter than honey to my mouth."

—Psalm 119:103

"Set your mind on things above, not on things on the earth."
—Colossians 3:2

"...For the LORD does not see as man sees; for man looks at the outward appearance, but the LORD looks on the heart."

—1 Samuel 16:7

"But immediately Jesus spoke to them saying, "Be of good cheer! It is I; do not be afraid."

—Matthew 14:27

"All your children shall be taught by the LORD; and great shall be the peace of your children."

—Isaiah 54:13

"Then Jesus spoke to them again, saying, "I am the light of the world. He who follows me shall not walk in darkness, but have the light of life."

—John 8:12

Printed in the United States
By Bookmasters